Grammar Girl's

101 Words Every High School Graduate Needs to Know

Also by Mignon Fogarty

Grammar Girl's Quick and Dirty Tips
for Better Writing

The Grammar Devotional

Grammar Girl Presents
the Ultimate Writing Guide for Students

Grammar Girl's 101 Misused Words
You'll Never Confuse Again

Grammar Girl's

101 Words Every High School Graduate Needs to Know

MIGNON FOGARTY

ST. MARTIN'S GRIFFIN 🐾 NEW YORK

GRAMMAR GIRL'S 101 WORDS EVERY HIGH SCHOOL GRADUATE NEEDS TO KNOW.
Copyright © 2011 by Mignon Fogarty, Inc. All rights reserved. Printed in
the United States of America. For information, address St. Martin's Press,
175 Fifth Avenue, New York, N.Y. 10010.

www.stmartins.com

Designed by Meryl Sussman Levavi

Illustrations by Arnie Ten

Library of Congress Cataloging-in-Publication Data

Fogarty, Mignon.
    Grammar Girl's 101 words every high school graduate needs to
know/Mignon Fogarty.—1st ed.
                p. cm.
    ISBN 978-0-312-57345-4
  1. Vocabulary.   2. English language—Terms and phrases.
I. Title.   II. Title: 101 words every high school graduate needs to know.
    PE1449.F557 2011
    428.1—dc22

                                              2011011240

First Edition: July 2011

10 9 8 7 6 5 4 3 2 1

Introduction

You may or may not have been taught these words in high school, but they'll serve you well from here on out. Use them in your college entrance essays or during job interviews to show that you're well-read and well-spoken. Even if you're past those stages in life, you'll regularly see most of these words in the news.

Since there are so many words that could legitimately be included in this book, for purely organization purposes, I've tried to adequately represent every letter of the alphabet; to spread the words over various disciplines such as politics, science, and economics; and to include some general vocabulary terms.

Ad Hoc

Ad hoc is literally Latin meaning "for this." We use *ad hoc* in English to describe something temporary, something that was created for a specific purpose or is a one-off. For example, an *ad hoc* decorations committee could be created for the sole purpose of organizing the prom decorations, and an *ad hoc* theme song meeting could be called to address the one specific issue of what theme song should be chosen. After their duties are fulfilled, the *ad hoc* committees disband and the *ad hoc* meetings adjourn.

> **It's my belief that [the CIA's] assassinations have always been** ad hoc **efforts, organized usually at the behest of policymakers above the agency—and usually unsuccessful.**
>
> —Aldrich Ames, CIA officer who spied
> for other countries,
> in William Safire's book
> *The Right Word in the Right Place
> at the Right Time*

Ad Hominem

Don't worry, the whole book won't be Latin, but the Latin *ad* word shows up a couple of times in important phrases. **Ad hominem** means "to the man" in Latin. We use it in English to describe a particular type of logical fallacy (see p. 30)—an argument that attacks the opponent's character instead of addressing the point of the debate.

An *ad hominem* attack assumes that just because a person is bad (e.g., a liberal, a conservative, a puppy killer) his or her argument can hold no merit, whereas in reality, a flawed person may still have a good point.

> **As we all felt keenly throughout the 2010 campaigns, name-calling and** ad hominem **attacks do more than insult the opponent: They insult the audience, as well.**
>
> —Margaret McDonald, American columnist

Anecdote

Anecdote comes from a Greek word that means "unpublished." *Anecdotes* are personal stories.

Anecdotes can be useful or deceptive depending on the situation; they can spice up a talk or supply the weak basis for a conclusion. For example, speaking coaches often encourage presenters to engage the audience by including amusing or compelling *anecdotes*. On the other hand, scientists often caution the public against making too much of mere *anecdotal* evidence such as the testimonials of a few happy supplement customers when there aren't any scientific studies proving the supplement works (or doesn't).

> **You know everything is not an** anecdote. **You have to discriminate. You choose things that are funny or mildly amusing or interesting. . . . Your stories have none of that. They're not even amusing accidentally!**
>
> —Steve Martin playing Neal Page (addressing Del Griffith) in the movie *Planes, Trains & Automobiles*

Antebellum

The next time you hear a Lady Antebellum song, remember that **antebellum** literally means "before the war" in Latin (*ante* = "before"; *bellum* = "war"). In the United States, *antebellum* usually refers only to the period before the Civil War; for example, you may read about *antebellum* architecture or *antebellum* collectibles that were made during this period. *The Old South* is sometimes used to describe the *antebellum* South, although *Old South* can also have a geographic or political meaning. (You're much more likely to hear about the *antebellum* South than about the *antebellum* North, since there were more changes in the South after the war.)

> **Cotton was king of the** antebellum **South, and befitting its regal position many retainers were necessary to bring each year's crop from the field to its ultimate destination in the North or abroad.**
>
> —Marilyn Anne Lavin in *William Bostwick, Connecticut Yankee in Antebellum Georgia*

Archetype

Archetype comes from a Greek word that means "an original," in the sense of an original mold, stamp, or template from which copies are made. *Archetype* is pronounced like *architect*—with a *ki* sound in the middle, not a *ch* sound.

In literature, an *archetype* is a type of character who appears in stories throughout the ages. The wise wizard (e.g., Gandalf from *Lord of the Rings,* Dumbledore from *Harry Potter*) and the hero who can wield a special weapon (e.g., King Arthur and the sword Excalibur, Luke Skywalker and the Jedi sword from *Star Wars*) are examples of *archetypes* that are often found in literature. Once you start looking for *archetypes,* you'll find them everywhere.

Archetype

Carl Jung popularized the *archetype* as a concept in psychology to represent ideas present in the collective unconscious.

> **I'm a man, Fleischman. We are born with an image of woman imprinted on our psyches. We spend our whole lives searching for the embodiment of that female** archetype. **And there she sits! In the flesh! You tell me what man could resist the fantasy of having her as his wife?**
>
> —Adam Arkin playing Adam in the TV show *Northern Exposure*

Austere

Something that is **austere** is simple, cold, harsh, or severe, especially in a way that limits pleasure or luxury. For example, an ascetic could be said to lead an *austere* life. A student's windowless room with only a simple bed and desk could be said to be *austere*.

Austere comes from Greek roots that mean "bitter, harsh, and dry" (as in how your mouth becomes parched). You can remember at least some of the meanings of *au<u>ster</u>ity* by noting that the *ster* in the middle is part of *<u>ster</u>n* and *<u>ster</u>ile*.

> **The truth is, there's nothing very utilitarian about fiction or its creation, and I suspect that people are desperate to make it sound like manly, back-breaking labor because it's such a wussy thing to do in the first place. The obsession with** austerity **is an attempt to compensate, to make writing resemble a real job, like farming, or logging.**

—Nick Hornby in *The Complete Polysyllabic Spree*

Banal

Something **banal** is common, mundane, trivial, or lacking originality. The word often carries a sense of how depressing it is to be confronted with such commonness. It comes from the Old French word *ban*, which described something that was common to the entire community.

> These memories . . . lay on the far side of a great divide in time, as significant as B.C. and A.D. Before prison, before the war, before the sight of a corpse became a banality.

—Ian McEwan, British writer, in *Atonement*

Banana's
$1.50

Bellicose

Bellicose means "warlike," so a *bellicose* person or country likes to fight.

In the *Star Wars* video games and books, an Empire star destroyer ship named *Bellicose* makes an appearance; and in the *Harry Potter* books, the violent and sadistic character Bellatrix Lastrange can trace her first name to the same Latin root word as *bellicose*—*bellum,* which means "war" and is also the root of *belligerent*. Think of Bellatrix Lastrange, and you've got a good way to remember the meaning of *bellicose*.

> **Chinese are losing patience with their erratic and** bellicose **ally [North Korea].**
>
> —William Pesek, Bloomberg News columnist, in an opinion piece for Bloomberg.

Blasphemy

Blasphemy is speaking or writing against something sacred or holy; for example, being irreverent about God is *blasphemy*. In early years, blasphemers were often put to death—and today, they still are in certain countries.

Blasphemy is an old word, coming to English from a Greek word with the same meaning. The *Oxford English Dictionary* shows Geoffrey Chaucer as the first English author to use the word with the 1384 line "In *blapheme* of the gods" in the poem *Lenvoy to Scogan* (actually an earlier version of the word: *blaspheme*). At first, *blasphemy* applied only to religious beliefs, but later its meaning expanded to include speaking against closely held secular beliefs too.

> **RANDAL GRAVES: Which did you like better? *Jedi* or *The Empire Strikes Back*?**
> **DANTE HICKS: *Empire.***
> **RANDAL GRAVES: Blasphemy.**
>
> —Jeff Anderson (Randal) and Brian O'Halloran (Dante) in the movie *Clerks*

Bohemian

You're most likely to hear **bohemian** used to describe fashion these days, but in addition to dress-up *bohemians*, there are also real *Bohemians*—people who come from the *Bohemian* region of the Czech Republic.

However, *bohemian* is also used to describe a philosophy or lifestyle that is now disconnected from the Bohemia region. The French, believing Gypsies (Romani) came to their country through Bohemia, were the first to use *bohemian* to describe Gypsy-like behavior—being carefree, unrooted, poor, and artistic, and generally embracing an unconventional or loose lifestyle. The word has since been applied to many different lifestyles and artistic communities that have some or all of these vague attributes.

> **Everything everybody does is so—I don't know—not wrong, or even mean, or even stupid necessarily. But just so tiny and meaningless and—sad-making. And the worst part is, if you go** bohemian **or something crazy like that, you're conforming just as much only in a different way.**
>
> —*Franny and Zooey* by J. D. Salinger

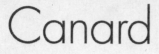

Canard

A **canard** is a story—usually a damaging story—that's false, but purports to be true. It can be a rumor, a hoax, or an out-and-out lie.

Canard also has specialized meanings in aeronautics and cooking, and the cooking part isn't surprising because *canard* literally means "duck" in French.

So how do we get from a word for ducks to an absurd, baseless rumor? Many dictionaries cite the origin as an old French expression to describe a scheme or a hoax that literally means "to sell half a duck." Clearly, you can't sell half a duck, or at least not half a live duck, so presumably the story is about a seller who cheated a buyer by selling less than a full fowl.

> **Don't you think it's odd that I, a dragon, should eat homework for lunch? Of course it's odd, for it never happened. It was a falsehood, a** canard, **a prevarication. Oh, why beat about the bush. It was a simple lie told by a little girl named Sandy.**
>
> —Burgess Meredith voicing Puff in the TV movie
> *Puff the Magic Dragon in the Land of Living Lies*

Chronic

Chronic relates to time—it describes something that is persistent or has been going on for a long time—and fittingly, it comes from a Greek word, *khronos,* that means "time." *Khronos* is also the root word for *chronology* and *chronically*—other words that relate to time.

In medicine, the opposite of a *chronic* disease (something that comes on slowly and will progress over a long time) is an acute disease (something that comes on suddenly, is severe, and is likely to end). For example, type II diabetes is a *chronic* condition and a stroke is an acute condition.

> **Speaking of** chronic **conditions, happy anniversary.**
>
> —Vivian Blaine playing Miss Adelaide
> in the movie *Guys and Dolls*

Correlation

When two things are *correlated,* they tend to happen together. A common scientific phrase is **correlation** *does not equal causation*—a reminder that studies often find that events happen at the same time without proving that one causes the other.

To use a silly example, it's important to remember that even though the girl you love seems to be scratching her head every time you walk by (the two events are *correlated*), you are not *causing* her to scratch her head. Perhaps your schedule means that you walk by at the same time she tends to study statistics, and it's statistics homework that makes her scratch her head.

> **The Lunar Effect is a myth. There is no statistical correlation between phases of the moon and human behavior.**
>
> —Pauley Perrette playing Abby Scuito in the TV show *NCIS: Naval Criminal Intelligence Service*

Crescendo

Crescendo comes from an Italian word that means "increasing." In a musical *crescendo*, the players gradually get louder until reaching a peak. Other things can also *crescendo*; political outrage can *crescendo*, romantic feelings can *crescendo*, a flurry of activity can *crescendo*, and a scene in a play can *crescendo*, for example.

Although it is sometimes used to describe a peak, technically, a *crescendo* is not *the* peak, but rather the lead-up to the peak.

Since the middle syllable of *crescendo* is pronounced "shen," I always had trouble remembering how to spell the word until I noticed that it's spelled like *descend*, which is something of its opposite in meaning.

> **A mosquito buzzed the King's ear with sudden** crescendo.
>
> —James Clavell in the novel *King Rat*

Deluge

Deluge means flood, and the word comes from a Latin root that means "to wash away." A *deluge* can be a real flood, as in a heavy downpour of rain, or a metaphorical flood, as in a *deluge* of paperwork that shows up on your desk when you get a new job or a deluge of leaves that fall on your lawn. It can also be a verb; for example, if you work in human resources, you could be the person *deluging* the new hire with paperwork.

> **Getting caught in the warm, wet** deluge **that particular day in that terrible summer full of wars and fires that made no sense was a wonderful thing to have happen. It taught me to understand rain,**

19

not to dread it. There were going to be days, I knew, when it would pour without warning, days when I'd find myself without an umbrella. But my understanding would act as my all-purpose slicker and rubber boots. It was preparing me for stormy weather, arming me with the knowledge that no matter how hard it seemed, it couldn't rain forever. At some point, I knew, it would come to an end.

—*Finding Fish: A Memoir* by
Antwone Quenton Fisher

Demagogue

Demagogue comes from a Greek word that means "the people's leader," but today in English it has a negative connotation. *Demagogues* seek to gain power, fame, money, or influence by inflaming an audience's emotions and prejudices with distortions and lies. *Demagogues* are usually persuasive speakers, and in short, they stir up trouble. *Demagogue* can also be used as a verb to describe the actions of such a person.

> **A public library is the most democratic thing in the world. What can be found there has undone dictators and tyrants:** demagogues **can persecute writers and tell them what to write as much as they like, but they cannot vanish what has been written in the past, though they try often enough. . . . People who love literature have at least part of their minds immune from indoctrination. If you read, you can learn to think for yourself.**
>
> —Doris Lessing, British Nobel laureate

Diatribe

Diatribe started as a Greek word that meant "to wear away time, study, or discourse" (the root words literally mean "to rub away") and came to English through Latin, where it had taken on the meaning "learned discourse." It originally held a similar meaning in English; however, in modern English use, *a diatribe* is negative—it's a bitter rant. Angry newspaper opinion pieces and political monologues on talk radio are often described as *diatribes*.

> [Winston Churchill] burst forth into an eloquent diatribe on the shortness of human life, the immensity of possible human accomplishment . . . in a torrent of magnificent language which appeared to be both effortless and inexhaustible and ended up with the words I shall always remember: "We are all worms. But I do believe that I am a glow worm."
>
> —Violet Bonham Carter, British politician

Disenfranchise

Enfranchise comes from an Old French word that means "to free." To **disenfranchise** is to take away a freedom or right.

In a political sense, people are *disenfranchised* when they cannot vote or their votes are not counted. You can't make it through a voting season without hearing about *disenfranchised* voters. More generally, to be *disenfranchised* can also mean to be denied some right or privilege, to be unrepresented, or to be shut out.

> **Literature is my Utopia. Here I am not** dis-enfranchised. **No barrier of the senses shuts me out from the sweet, gracious discourses of my book friends. They talk to me without embarrassment or awk-wardness.**
>
> —Helen Keller, deaf and blind American author

Eclectic

Eclectic comes from the Greek word for "selective." That may seem counterintuitive, since when someone says she has *eclectic* taste it means she likes a mix of styles, a hodgepodge, but it also means she is free to select whatever style works instead of being limited to just one. For example, someone who is *eclectic* is free to mix jazz, rock, and country music or free to select an Elizabethan bed and a French country dresser.

> Eclecticism **is the degree zero of contemporary general culture: one listens to reggae, watches a western, eats McDonald's food for lunch and local cuisine for dinner, wears Paris perfume in Tokyo and "retro" clothes in Hong Kong; knowledge is a matter for TV games. It is easy to find a public for eclectic works.**
>
> —Jean-François Lyotard, French philosopher

Elucidate

Elucidate's Latin root means "bright" or "to enlighten." To elucidate something is to figure it out, to metaphorically shine light on it. Scientists often speak of *elucidating* the mechanism behind some natural process, for example, *elucidating* the molecular mechanism that triggers an allergic reaction or *elucidating* the contribution of air pollution to heart disease.

Elucidate shares its Latin root with the word *lucid*, which means "clear minded." You can remember the meaning of *elucidate* by thinking that when you *elucidate* something it becomes clear (lucid) in your mind.

> **I remember scrutinizing his face. I remember drinking his face down to the last drop, trying to** elucidate **the character, the psychology of such an individual. And yet the only thing about him that has remained is my memory of his ugliness.**

> —*By Night in Chile* by Roberto Bolaño
> (translated by Chris Andrews)

Enmity

Enmity is the feeling you have toward an enemy: hatred, hostility, or ill will. I always had trouble remembering whether *n* or *m* came first until I linked the words <u>en</u>mity and <u>en</u>emy in my mind. (The word comes to English from Old French and Latin words that mean "enemy.")

When there's no evidence of another crime such as a robbery, police may speculate that the motive for murder is "personal *enmity*"—someone just hated the victims enough to kill them.

> It must be remembered that there is nothing more difficult to plan, more doubtful of success, nor more dangerous to manage, than the creation of a new system. For the initiator has the enmity of all who would profit by the preservation of the old institutions and merely lukewarm defenders in those who would gain by the new ones.
>
> —Niccolò Machiavelli, Italian philosopher

Epic

Maybe you've heard the word **epic** only in the slang phrase *epic fail* to describe a colossal disaster? Well, *epic* also has a literary meaning. For example, writers create *epic* poems and *epic* novels.

Epic works tend to be long, but that's not their only distinguishing characteristic. *Epic* poems and novels usually feature heroes facing challenges that will determine the fate of the world or have some other sweeping significance.

From these works, we get the meaning of *epic* that means "large or grand," as in *a project of epic proportions.*

Epic comes from a Greek word that means "story, narrative, poem, word, or song."

> **My mother was about to make another brilliant maneuver in the legendary battle of the lamp. The** epic **struggle which follows lives in the folklore of Cleveland Street to this very day.**
>
> —Jean Shepherd voicing the adult Ralphie in the movie *A Christmas Story*

Epitome

Epitome means the embodiment of something—a characteristic, a state, an emotion, or an ideal. If your room is the *epitome* of cleanliness, it represents everything that means cleanliness to the person who declared it so.

Epitome comes from a Greek word that means "to abridge or cut." It's a long stretch from *abridge* or *cut* to *embodiment,* but you can think of it this way: If you have to abridge or cut an entire novel down to just one paragraph, what you're left with is the single embodiment of the story, the one part that still transmits the meaning. In the same way, the *epitome* of cleanliness is the best representative of cleanliness after everything else has been cut.

You are the epitome **of everything I have ever looked for in another human being. And I know that you think of me as just a friend, and crossing that line is the furthest thing from an option you would ever consider. But I had to say it.**

—Ben Affleck playing Holden McNeil
in the movie *Chasing Amy*

Esoteric

An **esoteric** subject is uninteresting or hard to understand unless you're part of a select group. English classes such as "Allusions to Greek Mythology in Modern Literature" or math classes such as "Stochastic Processes" could be considered *esoteric* because they require an understanding of terms and theories that aren't well known in general society. *Esoteric* comes from a Greek word that means "inner" or "within," as in part of the inner circle or within the group.

> **Investors should be skeptical of history-based models. Constructed by a nerdy-sounding priesthood using** esoteric **terms such as beta, gamma, sigma and the like, these models tend to look impressive. Too often, though, investors forget to examine the assumptions behind the models. Beware of geeks bearing formulas.**
>
> —Warren Buffett, chairman and CEO of Berkshire Hathaway investment company

Fallacy

A **fallacy** is a lie or a commonly believed untruth. It comes from a Latin word that means "to deceive."

In the field of logic, a *fallacy* is a type of argument that makes the conclusion illogical. Common logical *fallacies* include appeals to authority, false dilemmas, straw man arguments, and ad hominem attacks (see p. 4).

People who give us their full confidence believe that they have thereby earned a right to ours. This is a fallacy; **one does not acquire rights through gifts.**

—Friedrich Nietzsche, German philosopher

Fascism

Benito Mussolini's regime, which led Italy into World War II, is considered to be the prototypical fascist government, and the word **fascism** comes into English from the Italian word *fascism,* which means "group" or "bundle" and was used by the Italians used to describe their political movement.

Fascism exists in different forms, but in general, fascist countries are headed by an all-powerful authoritarian leader and embrace war and patriotism as a way to keep

Fascism

the country unified and strong. Individual rights are abandoned in favor of the needs of the country. *Fascism* is strongly anticommunist and usually considered a far-right form of government. Inspired by Mussolini, Germany's World War II Nazi Party also instituted a *fascist* government.

Since the 1970s, *fascist* has also been used as an insult to describe someone who promotes any position in a militant or authoritarian manner (e.g., eco-*fascists*, airport TSA *fascists*, antitobacco *fascists*).

> **The only thing we hate more than bad manners is the goddamn** fascist **helmet law.**
>
> —John DeSantis playing Tiny
> in the TV show *Dead Like Me*

Firmament

Firmament refers to the heavens or the sky. It comes from a Hebrew word that means "expanse" and a Latin word that means "to support or make firm." You can think of the *firmament* as an expanse that holds the stars and planets firmly in space.

> **Large, heavy, ragged black clouds hung like crape hammocks beneath the starry cope of the night. You would have said that they were the cobwebs of the** firmament.
>
> —*The Hunchback of Notre Dame* by Victor Hugo

Fungible

Fungible means "interchangeable" or "able to be used in place of something else." For example, money is *fungible* because you can exchange it for other things (goods or other currencies), and sportswriters sometimes describe players as fungible because players have value and can be traded between teams.

Through its Latin root, *fungible* is related to the word *function,* so you can think of something that's *fungible* as something that functions as a commodity. If you want a more frivolous memory trick, you can think that *fungible* starts with *fun,* and it's fun to spend *fungible* things like money.

> **Experts explained how the corporate money that floods into a robust campaign is necessary and** fungible. **If such dollars cannot be spent in some states because of legal restrictions, they can be—and routinely are—swapped for money given by individual donors elsewhere that lack such restrictions.**
>
> —R. Jeffrey Smith, *Washington Post* staff writer, in a *Washington Post* article

Furlough

Furlough comes to English from a Dutch word that means "permission." Most commonly, a *furlough* is a temporary military leave, but it can also be used to describe the situation of workers who have been temporarily laid off. For example, a company or government agency with financial difficulties may *furlough* workers for a few days each month until the situation improves.

> **"Sir," said Mrs. Meade indignantly. "There are no deserters in the Confederate army."**
>
> **"I beg your pardon," said Rhett with mock humility. "I meant those thousands on** furlough **who forgot to rejoin their regiments and those who have been over their wounds for six months but who remain at home, going about their usual business or doing the spring plowing."**
>
> —*Gone with the Wind* by Margaret Mitchell

Galaxy

Our **galaxy**, what we now call the Milky Way, looks like a whitish stripe across the sky, and it was called many things throughout the ages, including the White Way and the Milky Circle. All this white milkiness is how we got the word *galaxy*: it comes from a Greek word for "milk," *gala*, which is also related to the words *lactose* and *lactate*. Chaucer was the first author we know of to commit *galaxy* to print.

The Milky Way *galaxy* is made up of many solar systems (planets, asteroids, and other objects that revolve around a sun), including the solar system that contains Earth. The reason we can see the Milky Way in the sky even though we are part of it is because our solar system is on the edge of the *galaxy*, so we're looking back through the rest of it. All the *galaxies* together make up the universe.

> **See yonder, lo, the** galaxy **which men call the Milky Way, for it is white.**
>
> —*The House of Fame* by Geoffrey Chaucer

Genocide

Genocide is the killing of an entire class of people such as a racial group or an ethnic group. When the Nazis tried to exterminate all the Jews during World War II, that was *genocide,* and sadly, it's not uncommon to read about attempted *genocide* in the news today.

Geno is from the Greek word for "race," and the suffix *-cide* means "to kill." Other *-cide* words include *homicide, pesticide, infanticide,* and *insecticide.*

> **While you were talking about organizing and committees, the extermination has already begun. Make no mistake, my brothers. They will draw first blood. They will force their cure upon us. The only question is, will you join my brotherhood and fight, or wait for the inevitable** geno- cide**? Who will you stand with—the humans or us?**
>
> —Ian McKellen playing Eric Lensherr
> in the movie *X-Men: The Last Stand*

Germane

Germane actually comes from the word *german*, but it has nothing to do with the country Germany. *German* meant "from the same parents," and Shakespeare gave it the metaphorical meaning it has today: something that is related, relevant, or important to the current topic or situation.

> **MARK SHUBB:** We give the audience a choice. We say, you can enjoy a toothpaste commercial, or do you wanna hear folk music?
>
> **JERRY PALTER:** I think they'll have already brushed their teeth by that time; it's not **even** germane.
>
> —Harry Shearer (Mark) and Michael McKean (Jerry) in the movie *A Mighty Wind*

Glacier

Glaciers are masses of ice, usually enormous, that are formed over many years in areas where snow falls and then flows downhill. *Glaciers* advance when snow accumulates and retreat when snow and ice melt. Both processes are usually slow, which has led to the use of *at a glacial pace* to mean "slowly." *Glaciers* can be so almost unfathomably large that their movement seems unrelenting, a meaning that is sometimes found in metaphorical uses of *glacier*.

Glacier comes from an Old French word for "ice": *glace*. Having trouble connecting *glace* and *ice*? Think of the simple icing for cakes called a glacé. (It's made by mixing powdered sugar and water.)

> **If, when you talk to people, they keep backing away from you, it's because you're too close, alright? So don't keep advancing on them like a human** glacier.

—Dave Barry, American humorist

39

Gregarious

A **gregarious** person enjoys the company of others and is happy in a crowd. The word comes from Latin for "part of the flock" as in a flock of birds, and it still has a specialized use in the sciences to describe animals that live in groups and plants that grow in open clusters.

> **At the times in my life when I was feeling the most** gregarious **and looking for bosom friendships, I couldn't find any takers, so that exactly when I was alone was when I felt the most like not being alone.**
>
> —Andy Warhol, American artist

Come to my house for lunch!

Harbinger

Harbinger comes from Old French and Old German words that meant "to provide shelter or lodging" and later had a sense of someone being sent ahead to arrange accommodations, and in that sense, _harbinger_ is related to the word _harbor_, as in "to shelter."

It is still used in English to describe someone who is sent ahead to arrange lodging or to announce an important person's arrival, but more often it is used metaphorically to describe a sign that foretells the coming of some person or event.

Although this memory trick isn't tied to the real roots of the words, you can think of a _harbinger_ as a bringer of things.

> **The true** harbinger **of spring is not crocuses or swallows returning to Capistrano, but the sound of the bat on the ball.**
>
> —Bill Veeck, owner of multiple Major League Baseball teams

Hegemony

Hegemony comes from a Greek word that means "leader or authority." Although it can be used outside of politics, *hegemony* is most commonly used to describe the power or dominance that one country or state has over others.

> **There has been talk in Europe about American** hegemony **being somehow based upon the use of the dollar in the world. I just don't see that connection at all.**
>
> —Robert C. Solomon, American professor

> **The** hegemony **of e-mail as a business medium is set to be superseded by social networking.**
>
> —Maxwell Cooter, *TechWorld* writer

Hemisphere

A **hemisphere** is half of a sphere or globe. Usually *hemisphere* refers to half the earth, such as the Northern *Hemisphere* or the Southern *Hemisphere,* but any roughly spherical item can be divided into *hemispheres,* and occasionally *hemisphere* will be used even more generally to describe an area of expertise or a realm.

In Greek, *hemi* means "half," and *sphere* comes from a Greek word that means "circle." You may be familiar with *hemi* because of advertisements for Hemi trucks. In those cases, *hemi* refers to the truck's engine, which has combustion chambers that look like bowls—the indentations that would be left by a *hemisphere.*

> **DR. ERIC FOREMAN: He probably just moved. Nobody stays perfectly still during those things.**
>
> **DR. GREGORY HOUSE: Right, he got uncomfortable and shifted one** hemisphere **of his brain to a more comfortable position.**
>
> —Omar Epps (Foreman) and Hugh Laurie (House) in the TV show *House*

Hubris

Hubris comes from Greek, where it originally meant "showing too much pride, self-confidence, or insolence to the gods." Today in English, *hubris* describes anyone who is arrogant or overly confident, whether or not the gods are involved.

> **"They didn't come to crush the city. They came to crush the hubris of its king."**
>
> **"That must have hurt," Oates said.**
>
> **Umber pinched the bridge of his nose.**
>
> **"Hubris means arrogance, you great buffoon."**
>
> —P. W. Catanese in the novel *Dragon Games*

Hypocrite

Hypocrite comes from Greek words that mean "an actor, a pretender" and "to feign." That makes perfect sense because *hypocrites* are people who feign to hold a belief or position. *Hypocrites* say they believe or cherish something, but take actions that are in conflict with those beliefs. For example, if someone campaigns against soda machines in schools for health reasons, but privately sells soda to students, that person is a *hypocrite*.

I remember that *hypocrite* is spelled with an *e* on the end by thinking, "*Hypocrites* make me say, 'Crikey!'" *Crikey* is an Australian exclamation of surprise or dismay that's pronounced "krahy-kee." The *e* sound on the end reminds me of the spelling.

> **You** hypocrite! Miss "grown-ups don't play with toys!" If I went into your apartment right now, would I not find Beanie Babies? Are you not an acquirer of Care Bears and My Little Ponies? And just who is that Japanese feline on your shorts? Hello, Hello Kitty!
>
> —Jim Parsons playing Sheldon Cooper in the TV show *The Big Bang Theory*

Impunity

Impunity has the same Latin root as *punitive* and *punish,* and translated, it literally means "without punishment." In English, *impunity* means "exempt from punishment, harm, or consequences" and often carries a sense of boldness or brazenness, a lack of fear of being caught or punished.

> **You look at these scattered houses, and you are impressed by their beauty. I look at them, and the only thought which comes to me is a feeling of their isolation and of the** impunity **with which crime may be committed there.**
>
> —Jeremy Brett playing Sherlock Holmes in the TV show *The Adventures of Sherlock Holmes*

Inflation

Inflation comes from a Latin word that means "to blow into," as in the way you'd blow into a balloon to inflate it. Politicians and bankers often talk about *inflation* in the monetary sense of the word. If governments rapidly blow money and credit into an economy, everyone has more money to spend, so money is less valuable and vendors raise their prices. That increase in what things cost is called *inflation*.

> **"Since we decided a few weeks ago to adopt the leaf as legal tender, we have, of course, all become immensely rich. . . ."**
>
> **"But we have also," continued the Management Consultant, "run into a small inflation problem on account of the high level of leaf availability, which means that, I gather, the current going rate has something like three deciduous forests buying one ship's peanut." . . .**

"So in order to obviate this problem," he continued, "and effectively revalue the leaf, we are about to embark on a massive defoliation campaign, and . . . er, burn down all the forests."

—*The Ultimate Hitchhiker's Guide to the Galaxy*
by Douglas Adams

Innocuous

Innocuous means "harmless, safe, or inoffensive"; it comes from a Latin prefix that means "not" and a root word that means "to harm." Often *innocuous* turns up in sentences to describe something that was thought to be harmless, but turned out to be dangerous, or something that is so dull and safe it's painful.

> **Apparently they died from overfeeding. Apparently I overfed them. Apparently fish are terrible gluttons with absolutely no self-control who just don't know when they've had enough and will stuff themselves to death with those** innocuous **little beige flakes imaginatively labeled "fish food."**
>
> *—A Fraction of the Whole*
> by Steve Toltz

Ironic

Irony is difficult to define, but you know it when you see it. What's **ironic** in one situation or to one person is not necessarily *ironic* in all situations or to all people because *irony* is related to the expected outcome or behavior. For example, a twelve-year-old girl wearing a pink tasseled hat is normal, but a fifty-year-old biker wearing a pink tasseled hat is *ironic*. It's all about what's expected.

Irony comes from the Greek word for "dissembler" and describes a situation in which something is the opposite of what you expect or what the speaker means.

> **It was** ironic, **really—you want to die because you can't be bothered to go on living—but then you're expected to get all energetic and move furniture and stand on chairs and hoist ropes and do complicated knots and attach things to other things and kick stools from under you and mess around with hot baths and razor blades and extension cords and electrical appliances and weedkiller. Suicide was a complicated, demanding business, often involving visits to hardware shops.**
>
> **And if you've managed to drag yourself from the bed and go down the road to the garden center or the drug store, by then the worst is over. At that point you might as well just go to work.**
>
> —*Lucy Sullivan Is Getting Married*
> by Marian Keyes

Jargon

Jargon originally described the sound made by chattering birds, and from that sense the meaning we know today evolved: specialized words (chattering) that outsiders don't understand. Most industries have their own jargon—shortcut words or phrases that everyone in the industry understands, but that are meaningless to anyone outside the industry—medical *jargon*, scientific *jargon*, art school *jargon*, and so on. Unless you're writing for an industry trade journal, avoid *jargon*.

> **Our business is infested with idiots who try to impress by using pretentious** jargon.
>
> —David Ogilvy, British advertising executive

Jeopardy

Jeopardy means "at risk or in danger." It comes from an Old French word that described a game with even odds; thus, the outcome was uncertain and either side was in danger of losing. It is almost always preceded by the word *in*: *They were in jeopardy*.

> **No matter how many times you save the world, it always manages to get back in jeopardy again. Sometimes I just want it to stay saved. You know, for a little bit? I feel like the maid; I just cleaned up this mess! Can we keep it clean for ten minutes?**
>
> —Craig T. Nelson voicing Mr. Incredible in the movie *The Incredibles*

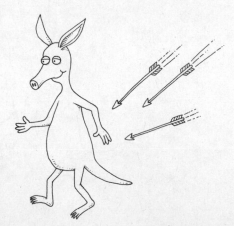

Judicious

Judicious means "showing good judgment, taking measured care." Someone who is *judicious* is wise, practical, sensible, prudent, and discreet. People can *judiciously* arrange guests at the table, *judiciously* choose their words, and *judiciously* trim their budgets.

Judicious comes from a Latin word for "judgment."

Advertising—a judicious **mixture of flattery and threats.**

—Northrop Frye, Canadian literary critic

Jurisdiction

Rarely can you watch a cop show without seeing two officers argue about who has **jurisdiction** over a case. *Jurisdiction* comes from Latin roots that mean "to say (*dictio*) the law (*juris*)." *Dictio* is also related to the English words *diction* and *dictate*.

A *jurisdiction* is an area over which an authority, such as a police department or a country, has legal control and the right to administer the law.

> **The offshore ocean area under U.S.** jurisdiction **is larger than our land mass, and teems with plant and animal life, mineral resources, commerce, trade, and energy sources.**
>
> —Tom Allen, American politician

Kibosh

A **kibosh** is something that silences, stops, or squelches something or someone.

The interesting thing about *kibosh* is that nobody knows where it came from; its origins are obscure—no Latin or Greek roots to talk about here. The earliest example of the word in the *Oxford English Dictionary* is from 1836, in which Charles Dickens used the phrase "put the *kibosh* on" someone, which is how you're still most likely to hear *kibosh* used today.

> One way to keep the [Eccentric Day] crowd limited is the one rule—you have to look eccentric to get in. . . . What if you're a little too eccentric? "A lot of people seem to think that being nude is eccentric enough," he said with a laugh. . . . "We had to put the kibosh on it," Reicherts said. Nudism is just not healthy in the cold of December.

> —Mark Wedel writing for
> the *Kalamazoo Gazette*

Kilometer

Outside the United States, almost everyone uses the metric system. People don't talk about how many miles they drove; they talk about how many **kilometers** they drove.

A meter is a distance a little more than a yard. *Kilo* means "thousand," so a *kilometer* is one thousand meters, which is a little more than half a mile (0.621 miles, to be exact). Other metric measurements include the centimeter (one-hundredth of a meter) and the millimeter (one-thousandth of a meter).

You'll most commonly encounter *kilometers* in the United States if you like to run in races. For example, if you participate in a "5K Fun Run," that's a five-kilometer race—a tad more than three miles.

> **Lisa, hello. How are you doing in England? Remember, an elevator is called a "lift," a mile is called a "kilometer," and botulism is called "steak and kidney pie."**
>
> —Julie Kavner voicing Marge Simpson in the TV show *The Simpsons*

Kudzu

Kudzu is an invasive, climbing, flowering vine that grows in the southeastern United States. If you're from the South, you're wondering who wouldn't know what *kudzu* is, but if you're not from the South, you may be baffled when you meet a southerner who describes something as "spreading like *kudzu*."

The plant is indigenous to China and Japan, and the name *kudzu* comes from its Japanese name.

> **In the world I see you are stalking elk through the damp canyon forests around the ruins of Rockefeller Center. You'll wear leather clothes that will last you the rest of your life. You'll climb the wrist-thick** kudzu **vines that wrap the Sears Towers.**

> —Brad Pitt playing Tyler Durden
> in the movie *Fight Club*

Laconic

From the Greek *Lakōn*, the name of a region near ancient Sparta. Laconians were known for their terse speech. The most famous example is the Laconian reply to Philip of Maceon's threat "If I enter Laconia, I will raze Sparta to the ground." Their ruler simply responded, "If."

In English, **laconic** is still used to describe someone of few words. It sometimes carries a negative connotation.

> **You can get far in North America with laconic grunts. "Huh," "hun," and "hi!" in their various modulations, together with "sure," "guess so," "that so?" and "nuts!" will meet almost any contingency.**
>
> —*For Your Eyes Only* by Ian Fleming, Scottish writer

Languish

To **languish** is to stay in a negative state without improving. People can *languish* in jail, *languish* with an illness or in a coma, *languish* in a bad relationship, or *languish* in college for ten years without choosing a major, for example. *Languish* comes from Latin words that mean "to be faint, weak, sick, or droopy." It's related to the words *languid, lax,* and *slack.*

Once upon a time, when I was a child reading fairy tales, I'd ached to have my own adventures. Not that I'd wanted to be some dippy heroine languishing in a tower, awaiting rescue. No, I'd wanted to be the knight, charging into battle against overwhelming odds, or the plucky country lass who gets taken on as

an apprentice to a great wizard. As I got older, I'd found out the hard way that adventures are rarely anything like the books say. Half the time you are scared out of your mind, and the rest you're bored and your feet hurt. I was beginning to believe that maybe I wasn't the adventurous type.

—*Claimed by Shadow* by Karen Chance

Largesse

Not surprisingly, **largesse** comes from an Old French root meaning "large." In English, it refers to generosity or extravagance, especially when it comes to money or gifts. It can describe the state of being generous (*Her largesse was legendary*) or the gifts themselves (*He's been living on his mother's largesse*). *Largesse* is the preferred spelling, but *largess* is also acceptable.

> **A democracy cannot exist as a permanent form of government. It can only exist until the voters discover that they can vote themselves** largesse **from the public treasury. From that moment on, the majority always votes for the candidates promising the most benefits from the public treasury with the result that a democracy always collapses over loose fiscal policy, always followed by a dictatorship. The average age of the world's greatest civilizations has been 200 years.**
>
> —Alexander Tyler, Scottish historian

Latitude

Latitude has both a scientific meaning and a general meaning. It comes from a Latin word that means "broad," which underlies both definitions.

On the globe, lines of *latitude* run horizontally, or broadly. *Latitude* is measured in degrees: the line on the equator is 0°, the North Pole is 90° north, and the South Pole is 90° south.

Outside of geography, *latitude* describes a state of freedom, the broad ability to make your own choices.

> **The teller of a mirthful tale has** latitude **allowed him. We are content with less than absolute truth.**
>
> —Charles Lamb, British essayist

Lethargy

People who are lethargic—suffering from **lethargy**—are dull and slow. For example, they may lie on the couch and ignore you when you enter the room, or they may show a general lack of interest in the world around them. *Lethargy* can be caused by illness or emotion, or may simply be someone's natural disposition. *Lethargy* comes from Greek words that mean "drowsy" and "forgetful."

> **JAMES HACKER: All we get from the civil service is delaying tactics.**
>
> **SIR HUMPHREY APPLEBY: Well, I wouldn't call civil service delays "tactics," Minister. That would be to mistake** lethargy **for strategy.**
>
> —Paul Eddington (Hacker) and Nigel Hawthorne (Appleby) in the British TV show *Yes Minister*

Malevolent

Malevolent comes from the Latin prefix *male-*, which means "evil" (sorry, guys!), and the root *volent*, which means "to will, wish, or desire," so someone who is malevolent wants bad things to happen.

We get the opposite word, *benevolent*, by putting the prefix *bene-*, which means "good," in front of the same root.

> **Americans are benevolently ignorant about Canada, while Canadians are ma-** levolently **well informed about the United States.**
>
> —John Bartlet Brebner, Canadian historian

Malignant

Malignant comes from the same Latin root word as *malign: malignari,* which means "malicious or spiteful." To malign someone is to speak ill of him. *Malign* sometimes carries a sense that the rumors are untrue.

Like being maligned, something *malignant* is very bad, whether it's a tumor, a situation, or a person.

Malignant diseases and situations are aggressive, out of control, and dangerous. In medicine, only *malignant* tumors are called cancer; less invasive tumors are called *benign. Malignant* people spread their evil and seek to harm others.

> **The once powerful,** malignant **Nazi state is crumbling.**
>
> —Franklin D. Roosevelt

Mandate

When you hear politicians talk about having a **mandate**, they mean the public has given them the authority, direction, or command to take some action. Within a governing structure, a superior ruler such a king or a pope can give a *mandate* to underlings or followers.

Mandate comes from a Latin word that means "command, order, or commission." It was a noun first and later became a verb. (Take that, all you people who complain about modern-day verbification of nouns.)

KING ARTHUR: The Lady of the Lake, her

Mandate

arm clad in the purest shimmering
samite, held aloft Excalibur from the
bosom of the water, signifying by divine
providence that I, Arthur, was to carry
Excalibur. That is why I am your king.

DENNIS: Listen, strange women lyin' in
ponds distributin' swords is no basis for
a system of government. Supreme exec-
utive power derives from a mandate
from the masses, not from some farcical
aquatic ceremony.

—Graham Chapman (King Arthur) and
Michael Palin (Dennis) in the movie *Monty Python
and the Holy Grail*

Meme

Meme is the youngest word you'll find in these pages; it was coined in 1976 by scientist Richard Dawkins in his book *The Selfish Gene*. He modeled *meme* on a Greek word that means "to copy" and meant for it describe an idea that is transmitted in much the same way as a gene.

Today, *meme* is often used to describe something that becomes popular or spreads quickly on the Internet. For example, LOLcats (cat pictures with funny captions such as *I can has cheezburger?*) are an Internet *meme*.

Meme

We need a name for the new replicator, a noun which conveys the idea of a unit of cultural transmission, or a unit of imitation. "Mimeme" comes from a suitable Greek root, but I want a monosyllable that sounds a bit like "gene." I hope my classicist friends will forgive me if I abbreviate mimeme to meme. . . . **It should be pronounced to rhyme with "cream." Examples of memes are tunes, ideas, catch-phrases, clothes fashions, ways of making pots or of building arches.**

—Richard Dawkins, Oxford professor,
in *The Selfish Gene*

Nadir

A **nadir** is a low point. It comes from an Arabic word that means "opposite to," and took its meaning from an Arabic phrase that meant "opposite to the zenith." (A zenith is a high point.) In English, a *nadir* can be a literal low point or a metaphorical low point such as an emotional or financial trough.

> **Mexico City's air pollution reached its nadir in 1991, when the city chalked up only eight days with air quality below hazardous levels.**
>
> —Tim Johnson in the *Miami Herald*

Nefarious

A **nefarious** act is evil, wicked, or villainous. Coming from a Latin prefix that means "not" followed by a root that means "divine law," *nefarious* has a sense of something that is against the law or is a deep offense against morality.

> **Worst of all, the majority of these dark criminals who had been caught in** nefarious **plots against the honour of France were totally unable to speak French.**

> —*The Enormous Room* by E. E. Cummings

Nepotism

Nepotism is showing favor to your relatives, especially in politics or the workplace. *Nepotism* comes from the Italian word for "nephew," which may seem strange until you learn that it acquired its current meaning during a time when Catholic popes regularly appointed their relatives, especially nephews, to powerful and lucrative positions.

> **It's not that I don't appreciate what you've done, but in this business, it's not courage that counts. It's** nepotism **that's important.**
>
> —Arte Johnson playing Sydney
> in the TV show *The A-Team*

Obliged

Obliged comes from a Latin word that means "to bind." It can be a synonym for "obligated" or "required" (*I'm* obliged *to tell you . . .* or *I'm obligated to tell you . . .*) or "in your debt" (*I'd be much* obliged *if you told me . . .*), but it can also mean "consented" (*He asked nicely, so I* obliged).

> **I'm going to kill you, Harry Potter. I'm going to destroy you. After tonight, no one will ever again question my power. After tonight if they speak of you, they'll only speak of how you begged for death. And how I, being a merciful Lord,** obliged.
>
> —Ralph Fiennes playing Lord Voldemort in the movie *Harry Potter and the Goblet of Fire*

Obtuse

In math, an **obtuse** angle is wider than 90 degrees and narrower than 180 degrees. It's the opposite of an acute angle. Since an acute angle is sometimes thought of as sharp, its opposite, the *obtuse* angle, is thought of as dull. In fact, *obtuse* comes from the Latin word for "dull."

When *obtuse* is used to describe a person, it also takes its clue from "dull." An *obtuse* person doesn't get your meaning, doesn't get the joke. He or she is stupid, slow, dimwitted, or dull.

> **CAPTAIN JEAN-LUC PICARD: You're going to deny us travel through space?**
>
> **Q: No, you** obtuse **piece of flotsam! You're to be denied existence. Humanity's fate has been sealed. You will be destroyed.**
>
> —Patrick Stewart (Picard) and John de Lancie (Q) in the TV show *Star Trek: The Next Generation*

Omniscient

Omniscient comes from the Latin word for "all-knowing," and someone who is *omniscient* has godlike knowledge of everything.

In literature, books are sometimes described as having an *omniscient* narrator, also known as an *omniscient* third-person narrator. In such stories, the narrator can report on the actions and thoughts of every character and on events beyond the realm or awareness of the characters—in short, on anything. (It is also possible to have a *limited* third-person narrator who knows the thoughts and actions of one or a few characters in the book, but doesn't have sweeping knowledge of the world or all the characters as an *omniscient* narrator would.)

BIG BROTHER: Let me explain something here. Big Brother is a name we use to suggest an omniscient **totalitarian presence. It's not supposed to be taken literally. I'm your oppressor, not your friend.**

CITIZEN 43275-B: But is says in the re-education manual that Big Brother is our friend.

BIG BROTHER: That's just empty political propaganda. It doesn't mean . . . It doesn't mean I wanna hear your stupid knock knock jokes.

—Dan Kern (Big Brother) and Michael Naughton (Citizen 43275-B) in the short movie *Me and the Big Guy*

Onerous

Onerous comes from a Latin word that means "burden," and today in English it still means "burdensome" as well as "oppressive or troublesome." You can remember the meaning by linking the *one* part of <u>one</u>*rous* with the idea that all the weight is a burden on one person's shoulders, like the famous sculpture of Atlas holding the whole world on his shoulders.

> **The Electric Monk was a labour-saving device, like a dishwasher or a video recorder. . . . Electric Monks believed things for you, thus saving you what was becoming an increasingly onerous task, that of believing all the things the world expected you to believe.**
>
> —*Dirk Gently's Holistic Detective Agency* by Douglas Adams

Ordinance

Ordinance comes from a Latin word that means "to arrange," and it refers to a law, rule, or regulation.

Ordinance should not be confused with *ordnance*— military items for shooting such as artillery, cannons, ammunition, missiles, bombs, and the supplies needed to maintain these items. *Ordinance* used to include these items, but *ordnance* evolved into its own term. You can think that when people are at war using ordnance, they're in a hurry and not focused on spelling, so they dropped the *i* for convenience.

> **Under any conditions, anywhere, whatever you are doing, there is some** ordinance **under which you can be booked.**
>
> —Robert D. Specht, distinguished mathematician

Penultimate

Penultimate is often mistakenly used to hyperbolically describe something as better than the best, but it properly means "the next to last." *Penultimate* comes from a Latin word that means "almost ultimate." The next to last book in a series, the next to last day of a vacation, and the next to last game in a player's career are all *penultimate* items or events.

> **Believe me, ladies and gentlemen, there is nothing** penultimate **about this one. This, ladies and gentlemen, is the proverbial it. After this, there is void . . . emptiness . . . oblivion . . . absolute nothing.**
>
> **[dramatic pause]**
>
> **Except, of course, for the sweets trolley and our fine selection of Aldebaran liqueurs. And for once, ladies and gentlemen, there is no need to worry about having a hangover in the morning, for there will be no more mornings.**
>
> —Colin Jeavons playing Max Quordlepleen in the TV miniseries *A Hitchhiker's Guide to the Galaxy*

Plagiarize

I always had trouble remembering how to spell **plagiarize** until I realized that the middle part is spelled like *liar*: A *plag<u>iar</u>izer* is a <u>liar</u>.

To *plagiarize* is to use someone else's words or ideas without a proper citation, usually with the intent to pass them off as your own, so the "liar" memory trick fits.

The first English word related to *plagiarize* is *plagiary*, which came from a Latin word that described a person who kidnaps, seduces, or plunders.

In British English it is spelled with an *s* instead of a *z*: *plagiarise*.

> **OK, maybe my dad did steal Itchy. So what? Animation is built on** plagiarism. **If it weren't for someone plagiarizing The Honeymooners we wouldn't have The Flintstones.**
>
> —Alex Rocco voicing Roger Meyers Jr.
> on the TV show *The Simpsons*

Poignant

Something **poignant** is painfully moving, keenly felt, or sharply experienced. *Poignant* comes from a Latin word that meant "to prick" and a later Old French word that meant "to prick or sting" and may be related to the word *pungent,* which has a similar meaning but is more likely to be applied to a taste or a smell.

> **What I heard then was the melody of children at play. Nothing but that. And I knew that the hopelessly** poignant **thing was not Lolita's absence from my side, but the absence of her voice from that chorus.**
>
> —Jeremy Irons playing Humbert Humbert in the movie *Lolita*

Profligate

A **profligate** man is shamelessly corrupt, wanton, or recklessly extravagant. For example, *profligate* liars not only lie, but do it all the time and don't feel bad about it. They may even enjoy lying. *Profligate* comes from a Latin word that meant, among other things "ruined, depraved, or corrupt."

> **If, in looking at the lives of princes, courtiers, men of rank and fashion, we must perforce depict them as idle, profligate, and criminal, we must make allowances for the rich men's failings, and recollect that we, too, [would be] very likely indolent and voluptuous, had we no motive for work, a mortal's natural taste for pleasure, and the daily temptation of a large income.**
>
> —William Makepeace Thackeray, British novelist

Pugnacious

A **pugnacious** person likes to fight in a "Bring on the argument; I'm itching for a quarrel!" kind of way.

Pugnacious comes from a Latin root that means "combative," which is, in turn, related to a Greek word that means "fist." If it helps, remember that *pugnacious* means "belligerent" by imagining a feisty pug dog that's raring for a fight.

> **[Conor] Casey was** pugnacious **from the start and combative throughout. His spirit—and his goal—lifted the Rapids, who managed to come back from an initial deficit only once in 12 games this season.**
>
> —Jeffrey Marcus in the *New York Times*

Quadrant

Quadrant comes from Latin words that mean "the fourth part," and a *quadrant* is defined as one quarter of a circle. If you had a pie (cherry, chocolate, pecan—any pie will do) and cut it in half, and then cut each of those pieces in half, you'd have four equal slices, and one slice would be a *quadrant* of the pie.

> **DR. GREGORY HOUSE:** As I suspected, you have significant losses in the upper right quadrant **of your visual field.**
>
> **EVAN GREER:** Are you serious?
>
> **DR. GREGORY HOUSE:** No, it's a joke. Two guys go into a bar and one has significant losses in the upper right quadrant of his visual field. And the other one says, "You're gonna need an MRI to confirm the type and location of the tumor."
>
> —Hugh Laurie (House) and Jason Lewis (Greer) in the TV show *House*

Quantitative

Quantitative comes from the Latin word for "quantity." *Quantitative* analysis looks at things that can be measured, such as the number of dolphins in a region. *Qualitative* analysis looks at things that are more subjective, such as how seeing dolphins made tourists feel. *Qualitative* analysis is more prone to problems with the wording of the question or other things that may subtly bias the participants.

People often confuse *quantitative* and *qualitative,* in part because qualitative results can be presented in ways that makes them look *quantitative,* for example, when researchers ask qualitative questions, but have subjects answer on numerical scales: *How happy were you to see dolphins? Answer on a scale from 1 to 10.*

> **We measure the success of schools not by the kinds of human beings they promote but by whatever increases in reading scores they chalk up. We have allowed**

quantitative **standards, so central to the adult economic system, to become the principal yardstick for our definition of our children's worth.**

—Kenneth Keniston, American professor of human development

Quixotic

Quixotic comes from the name of the literary character Don Quixote from Miguel de Cervantes's novel *The Ingenious Hidalgo Don Quixote of La Mancha* (bonus word—a hidalgo is a lower nobleman in Spain), so someone who is *quixotic* has the characteristics of Quixote—romantic, overly chivalrous, extravagant, foolish, rash, and impractical. (Reading the book will help you understand the word better!)

Even though *quixotic* is derived from Don Quixote's name, it is pronounced differently because the word *quixotic* is an Anglicization of the name. It is pronounced "kwik-*sot*-ik," whereas the name is still pronounced much like the original Spanish: "kee-*hoh*-tee."

> **All male friendships are essentially** quix-otic: they last only so long as each man is willing to polish the shaving-bowl helmet, climb on his donkey, and ride off after the other in pursuit of illusive glory and questionable adventure.
>
> —*Wonder Boys* by Michael Chabon

Rancor

Rancor is a feeling of hate, bitterness, hostility, or spite. It comes from a Latin word that has a sense of a bad smell or rankness and is also a root of the word *rancid*.

In Britain, it's typically spelled *rancour*.

> **Amazing how grimly we hold on to our misery, the energy we burn fueling our anger. Amazing how one moment, we can be snarling like a beast, then a few moments later, forgetting what or why. Not hours of this, or days, or months, or years of this . . . But decades. Lifetimes completely used up, given over to the pettiest** rancor **and hatred. Finally, there is nothing here for death to take away.**

> —Matt Dillon playing Henry Chinaski
> in the movie *Factotum*

Recession

Recession comes from a Latin word that means "to recede," and has many meanings tied to that root, but the one you're most likely to encounter is the kind of *recession* that occurs in an economy. A *recession* is, in a sense, when an economy recedes from plenty. Unemployment goes up, while spending, production, and income go down.

Many sources define a *recession* vaguely—as simply a move in this downward direction, or as a downturn less severe than a depression—but in the 1970s, some economists began to quantify the term, defining it as two consecutive quarters in which the gross domestic product falls. (Gross domestic product, also known as GDP, is the value of the goods and services a country produces.)

Recession started being used to describe economic conditions around the beginning of the period that later became known as the Great Depression, presumably because at first people didn't realize how bad it was going to get.

**It's a recession when your neighbor loses
his job; it's a depression when you lose
your own.**

—Harry Truman, American president

Redress

Redress comes from an Old French word that meant "to straighten again," and today it means "to provide justice, relief, a remedy, or compensation; to right a wrong." *Redress* is a more general term than *reparation* (a financial remedy) or *restitution* (putting things back as they were before a wrong was committed).

> **You can't just lecture the poor that they shouldn't riot or go to extremes. You have to make the means of legal** redress **available.**
>
> —Harold H. Greene, American judge

Rhetoric

Rhetoric is the ability to use language persuasively. Excellence at *rhetoric* can be seen as a noble, valued skill or merely as a way with deception, depending on the ends to which rhetoricians use their linguistic art.

There are easily more than a hundred different *rhetorical* devices; some of the simplest include word patterns known to engage audiences, such as alliteration (using words that start with the same sounds: *Let us go forth to lead the land we love*—John F. Kennedy's inauguration speech) and repetition (*Yes, we can*—repeated seven times in Barack Obama's presidential victory speech).

> **Everyone was tired with the old style politicians and their flowery** rhetoric. **I just told them there are tough times ahead, but that they would be less tough with me in charge.**
>
> —Aníbal Cavaco Silva, president of the Portuguese Republic

Romance

I bet you know what **romance** means, but what about *Romance*? French, Italian, Spanish, and Portuguese aren't called *Romance* languages because they are the languages of love; they're called *Romance* languages because they all can be traced back to Vulgar Latin, the informal, spoken language of Rome. (Classical Latin was the written language used by educated Romans.)

The similarities between Latin and Ro- mance **languages are easy to see, and students of Latin will notice thousands more if they study a Romance language as well.**

Latin	pater
French	pere
Spanish	padre
Italian	padre
Portuguese	pai

—*Ancient Rome: An Introductory History*
by Paul A. Zoch

Sanguine

Sanguine means "cheerfully optimistic or confidently hopeful" and is sometimes used to describe the happy disposition of youth.

Sanguine comes from a Latin word that means "bloody," which may seem strange at first, but back in the 1500s when *sanguine* took on its "happy disposition" meaning, people thought that personality traits, such as sanguinity, came from the four humors, one of which was blood. (The other three humors were yellow bile, black bile, and phlegm.)

> **No temper could be more cheerful than hers, or possess in a greater degree that** sanguine **expectation of happiness which is happiness itself.**
>
> —Jane Austen, describing Mrs. John Dashwood
> in *Sense and Sensibility*

Sans

Sans is a foreign-sounding or old-timey way of saying "without." It comes from French and Latin words with the same meaning and was popular in Shakespeare's time.

You may encounter *sans* in the font description *sans serif.* Serifs are the little extensions that appear on the end of lines and curves in fonts such as Times New Roman and Georgia (T, T) and *sans serif* literally means "without serif." Sans serif fonts such as Helvetica and Arial lack the artistic projections at the ends of the lines and curves (T, T).

> **I've been to New York. It's like Prague** sans **the whimsy.**
>
> —Seth MacFarlane voicing Brian Griffin
> in the TV show *Family Guy*

Sartorial

Sartor is the Latin word for "tailor," so its derivative, **sartorial**, refers to clothes. It's regularly used in news stories describing fashion.

> **A true Scotsman is said to never wear anything under his kilt. But now Scots are being warned that the** sartorial **tradition could be both indecent and unhygienic.**
>
> —Ben McConville in a story for the Associated Press

Schadenfreude

Schadenfreude is a German word that combines "harm" and "joy." It's the feeling you get when you take pleasure in someone else's misfortune. *Schadenfreude* has been used in English for many years, but it seemed to experience a slight increase in use after being defined in a 1991 episode of *The Simpsons* ("When Flanders Failed"), and then a burst in use around the time of the dot-com bust, perhaps because so many people took pleasure in seeing twenty-year-old overnight millionaires brought down a notch. The word received more support when the musical *Avenue Q* premiered on Broadway in 2003 and included a song titled "*Schadenfreude.*"

> **Winter denial: therein lay the key to California** Schadenfreude—**the secret joy that the rest of the country feels at the misfortune of California. The country said: "Look at them, with their fitness and their tans, their beaches and their movie stars, their Silicon Valley and silicone breasts, their orange bridge and their palm trees. God, I hate those smug, sunshiny bastards!" Because if you're up to your navel in a**

snowdrift in Ohio, nothing warms your heart like the sight of California on fire. If you're shoveling silt out of your basement in the Fargo flood zone, nothing brightens your day like watching a Malibu mansion tumbling down a cliff into the sea.

—*The Stupidest Angel: A Heartwarming Tale of Christmas Terror* by Christopher Moore

Shrewd

Shrewd used to be a much more negative term than it is today. It comes from a Middle English word that meant "to curse" and it was associated with evil. Today, however, someone who is *shrewd* is tough, sharp, informed, insightful, and astute—a worthy competitor. You may not enjoy a day at the park with someone who is *shrewd,* but you'd want him or her on your side in a negotiation, and if you have to go up against someone who is shrewd, you'd better be on your toes.

> **We're faced with a shrewd and ruthless gang of outlaws. Their operation is clever and deadly. They wait until a man with a price on his head is jailed, then spring him and use him as a front man for a series of holdups . . . making sure he is the only one ever recognized. The reward keeps going up. When it reaches three or four thousand dollars, the man is killed. Somebody is hired to collect the reward.**
>
> —Thomas Browne Henry playing Mike O'Brien in the movie *Gunfight at Comanche Creek*

Solstice

A **solstice** occurs when the sun is farthest from the equator; it happens twice a year, once in summer and once in winter. In the Northern Hemisphere, the summer *solstice* has the most daylight of the year and the winter *solstice* has the least daylight of the year.

Solstice comes from a Latin word that means "to stand still" because on a *solstice,* the sun stops moving in the direction it has been moving. For example, in the Northern Hemisphere, each day the sun will gradually move northward in the sky until the summer *solstice,* after which the sun will begin to move southward—until the winter *solstice,* when it will switch again.

Civilizations have often treated *solstices* as important or sacred days.

> **We were raised on lentils, brown rice, Neil Young, and** solstice **celebrations.**
>
> —*Vanishing and Other Stories* by Deborah Willis

Sovereignty

Sovereignty is control or power over something, often a country or larger geographical region, but it can also be used in a limited sense to describe an individual having control over his or her body or home. It has more of a sense of independence or autonomy when used in this manner. *Sovereignty* comes from a Latin word that means "over" as in "to reign over."

Sovereignty has the word *reign* in the middle, so connect it in your mind to the idea of a king reigning over his lands.

The moon and other celestial bodies should be free for exploration and use by all countries. No country should be permitted to advance a claim of sovereignty.

—Lyndon B. Johnson, American president

Sufficient

Sufficient means "enough," and it comes from a Latin word that means "to make," as in "to make do" with something. In the phrase *self-sufficient*, *sufficient* means "reliant"—that the person is able to take care of himself or herself.

Scientists often talk about the difference between things being necessary and things being *sufficient*. To use a cooking example, flour is necessary to make bread, but it is not *sufficient*. Minimally, you also need water with your flour to make the simplest kind of unleavened bread. Together, water and flour are *sufficient*—enough. It won't be the tastiest bread in the world, but it will be bread.

> **Toby:** I'd probably be, like, disemboweled by a ninja.
>
> **Bree Osbourne:** You don't have to say "like." "Probably disemboweled by a ninja" is *sufficient*. And please don't put your feet up on the dashboard.
>
> —Kevin Zegers (Toby) and Felicity Huffman (Bree) in the movie *Transamerica*

Taciturn

Taciturn and *tacit* are both adjectives that come from a Latin word that means "silent." *Taciturn* is usually used to describe people, and *tacit* is usually used to describe a situation or state. *Taciturn* people are quiet and reserved—they don't speak a lot and may be considered dour or grumpy. *Tacit* often means "implied" or "unspoken." For example, a *taciturn* man may give *tacit* permission for his daughter to go out Friday night by simply shrugging instead of saying "Yes, you can go."

> **Her laugh was sad and** taciturn, **seemingly detached from any feeling of the moment, like something she kept in the cupboard and took out only when she had to, using it with no feeling of ownership, as if the infrequency of her smiles had made her forget the normal way to use them.**
>
> —Gabriel García Márquez, Colombian author and Nobel laureate in *Leaf Storm*

Tangent

Tangent has a conversational meaning and a math meaning, both of which relate to its Latin root—a word that means "to touch."

In geometry, a *tangent* is a line that touches one point on a curve. Outside of math, a *tangent* is an idea or a line of reasoning that goes off in an unrelated or unexpected direction. Just as in math, the topic starts at a point on the conversational "curve" and then proceeds in a different direction.

> **The other day in my positive psychology class I was talking about oxytocin—AKA the cuddle hormone—and its social benefits. Oxytocin is stimulated by human touch, and I believe research has shown a similar effect from contact with pets. I suppose that's why we call them pets— because we can and do pet them. I went off on a** tangent **about why turtles and goldfish are not pets in the literal sense. My students chuckled a bit, and then one of them asked a great question. "What about teddy bears?"**
>
> —Christopher Peterson on the
> *Psychology Today* blog

Tenacious

Something **tenacious** has a strong grip either physically or metaphorically. Dough can stick *tenaciously* to a rolling pin, a person can stick *tenaciously* to a task, and a child can cling *tenaciously* to his mother on the first day of preschool.

Tenacious comes from a Latin word that means "holding fast."

> **Metaphors are much more** tenacious **than facts.**
>
> —Paul de Man, Belgian philosopher

Trepidation

Although **trepidation** no longer requires a sense of trembling, it originally came from the Latin word that meant "to tremble, to be agitated, to be alarmed, or to hurry."

The *Oxford English Dictionary* shows the first use of the word in 1605 by Francis Bacon in a piece on scientific

Should I touch it?

philosophy. At that time, it still had its "trembling" meaning: *Massive bodies have certain* trepidations *and wavering, before they fix and settle.*

Today, *trepidation* still means "a feeling of fearfulness, anxiety, or agitation"; but the *trepidatious* person need not be quaking.

> **Being at the center of a film is a burden one takes on with innocence—the first time. Thereafter, you take it on with** trepidation.
>
> —Daniel Day-Lewis, British and Irish actor

Ubiquitous

An old joke goes something like this: "**Ubiquitous**? I keep seeing that word everywhere." It's funny (or trying to be funny) because *ubiquitous* comes from a Latin root that means "everywhere," and it still means "everywhere" in English. Something *ubiquitous* is so pervasive that it's nearly unavoidable—like pollen on a spring day or Starbucks.

> **Music and light spilled out of so many grand houses that the two seemed at once** ubiquitous **and united, as if to play a note was to send forth a ray of illumination, and a quartet was enough to set the grandest halls aglitter.**
>
> —*The Magicians and Mrs. Quent* by
> Galen M. Beckett

Unwieldy

The root of **unwieldy** is *wield,* which means "to handle" (as in a weapon) or "to control" (as in power) and comes from many old words that meant "to rule." Therefore, something that is *unwieldy* is difficult to handle, whether it's an unwieldy people who are difficult to rule, *unwieldy* emotions that are difficult to process, or an *unwieldy* sword that is hard to manage gracefully.

> **Our houses are such** unwieldy **property that we are often imprisoned rather than housed by them.**
>
> —Henry David Thoreau, American author

Usurp

Usurp comes from a Latin word that meant "to use or seize" and in English still means "to seize," as in to seize power from another in an illegal way such as through a coup, a mutiny, or an uprising. In olden times, a *usurper* may have also tried to take the throne by guile while a monarch was away from the kingdom.

> It was not because the three-penny tax on tea was so exorbitant that our Revolutionary fathers fought and died, but to establish the principle that such taxation was unjust. It is the same with this woman's revolution; though every law were as just to woman as to man, the principle that one class may usurp the power to legislate for another is unjust, and all who are now in the struggle from love of principle would still work on until the establishment of the grand and immutable truth, "All governments derive their just powers from the consent of the governed."
>
> —Susan B. Anthony, American suffragist

Visage

Visage comes from a Latin word meaning "appearance" and an Old French word meaning "face" and today can refer to a face, a temperament showing on a face, a likeness, or a general outward appearance.

> **O conspiracy,**
> **Sham'st thou to show thy dangerous brow**
>   **by night,**
> **When evils are most free? O then, by day**
> **Where wilt thou find a cavern dark**
>   **enough**
> **To mask thy monstrous** visage?

—Brutus in William Shakespeare's *Julius Caesar*

Wag

You're certainly familiar with the image of a dog wagging its tail or gossips wagging their tongues, but **wag** has another meaning—a name for a kidder or mischievous jokester. Dictionary makers are uncertain whether the meaning evolved from the verb *wag* and the image of a playful dog or the obscure English word *waghalter*, which described someone who was likely to hang from the halter (gallows).

> **Hello. I am Homer Simpson. Or as some of you** wags **have dubbed me, Father Goose.**
>
> —Dan Castellaneta voicing Homer Simpson in the TV show *The Simpsons*

Wallow

Wallow comes from an Old English word that meant "to roll." Pigs wallow in the mud—they roll and linger in it. Today, *wallow* means "to linger in an emotional state or to dwell on something too long." Like the pigs, people who are *wallowing* are self-indulgently rolling around in their emotions. Although you can use *wallow* to describe lingering in a happy place (*wallowing* in the love of my family), it's much more commonly used to describe extended dwelling on negative emotions—moping.

> **The nerve of those Whos. Inviting me down there on such short notice! Even if I wanted to go, my schedule wouldn't allow it. 4:00, wallow in self pity; 4:30, stare into the abyss; 5:00, solve world hunger, tell no one; 5:30, Jazzercize; 6:30, dinner with me—I can't cancel that again; 7:00, wrestle with my self-loathing. I'm booked.**
>
> —Jim Carrey playing
> the Grinch in the movie
> *How the Grinch Stole Christmas*

Xeriscape

Please, never call a yard that requires little water a *ze-roscape*; it's **xeriscape**, which comes from a combination of the Greek word *xeric*, meaning "having scant moisture," and the word *scape*, which in this case refers to a type of land. I can see why people get confused and think the word is *zeroscape*, because a *xeriscape* requires almost zero maintenance, but according to the *Oxford English Dictionary*, the word was coined by the Denver Water Department in 1981—and the word is *xeriscape*.

The root *xeric* in *xeriscape* comes from the Greek prefix *xer-*, which means "dry." There aren't many English words that use the *xer-* prefix. *Xeroderma* is dry skin, *xerography* is a type of dry printing, and *xerophagy* is eating dry food. There are few others.

> **In some ways,** xeriscaping **is a return to normal for desert communities.**
>
> —*Greening Your Home: Sustainable Options for Every System in Your House*, by Clayton Bonnett

Yiddish

Yiddish is a language spoken in Jewish communities, and the name comes from the German word for Jewish (*jüdisch*). High German is considered to be the root language of *Yiddish*, although *Yiddish* is written with Hebrew characters and, like English, has also incorporated aspects of many other languages, including Hebrew and Romance and Slavic languages.

Some have debated whether *Yiddish* is an autonomous language or simply a German dialect. This debate led to the famous quotation cited in a Max Weinreich lecture, "A language is a dialect with an army and a navy." *Yiddish* words you might already know include *chutzpah* ("nerve"), *klutz* ("clumsy person"), *shmutz* ("a little dirt"), and *oy vey* (exclamation of exasperation).

> **In a corner of the yard lay a pile of smashed stones on which appeared inscriptions in Hebrew and sometimes** Yiddish. **These were all that remained of the gravestones. There wasn't a Jew left in the town, and there hadn't been one, said Mr. Kichler, since 1945.**
>
> —*Hitch-22: A Memoir* by Christopher Hitchens

Zeal

Zeal is a disposition or an attitude, an enthusiastic or fervent devotion to a purpose. It often has a negative connotation. For example, a *zealot* (a word derived from *zeal*) is usually seen as someone who takes things to an irrational extreme—acts in a fanatical way.

Zeal comes from a Greek word that also meant "zeal."

> **Most of the major ills of the world have been caused by well-meaning people who ignored the principle of individual freedom, except as applied to themselves, and were obsessed with fanatical** zeal **to improve the lot of mankind-in-the-mass through some pet formula of their own.**
>
> —Ezra Taft Benson, American statesman and religious leader, in the speech "The Proper Role of Government"

Acknowledgments

I am especially indebted to the sources I used in my research, including Great Quotes (great-quotes.com), the Internet Movie Database (IMDB.com), the Quotations Page (quotationspage.com), the Quotation section at Dictionary.com (http://quotes.dictionary.com/, based on *The Columbia World of Quotations*), Google Books, and all the people who have highlighted favorite quotations in the Good Reads Quotation section (http://www.goodreads.com/quotes). For etymology research and definitions, I relied primarily on the online versions of the *Oxford English Dictionary, second edition; Webster's Third New International Dictionary, Unabridged*, and on Dictionary.com. Finally, a special thanks to @StolenDay on Twitter for pointing me to a blog post by Andy Bechtel, a copy editor

Acknowledgments

who teaches at the School of Journalism and Mass Communication at the University of North Carolina, Chapel Hill, which discusses the 1991 use of *schadenfreude* in *The Simpsons*.

Thank you also to Lisa Senz at St. Martin's Press, Emily Rothschild and Richard Rhorer at Macmillan, and Laurie Abkemeier at DeFiore and Company. Finally, most of all, thank you to my husband, Patrick. I'm glad we both took that English 101 course our senior year, and that the most convenient empty seat was next to you.

About the Author

Mignon Fogarty is the creator of Quick and Dirty Tips. Formerly a magazine writer, technical writer, and entrepreneur, she has a B.A. in English from the University of Washington in Seattle and an M.S. in biology from Stanford University. She lives in Reno, Nevada. Visit her Web site at quickanddirtytips.com and sign up for the free e-mail grammar tips and free podcast.